Train Your
MIND
To Think
POSITIVE

Also by Benson N. MODIE:

1. The Wisdom of The Evolving Species: *inspired words to ignite your personal growth*.
2. The Voice of BENMOD TheEvolvingSpecies: *thoughts, ideas, views and opinions to help you manage yourself in life*.
3. Effective Living: *a guide to self-fulfilment*.
4. A Guide to Effective Life Planning: *how to make the most out of your moment in life*.
5. The Future I Desire: *a step in evolution*.
6. Words of Wisdom: *120 motivational tips to inspire you to greatness*.

Train Your
MIND
To Think
POSITIVE

Thought Patterns To Help You
Create The Conditions Of
Peace, Love, Joy And Happiness
In Your Life

Benson N. Modie
B.Sc., M.Phil., Ph.D.

The Centre for Knowledge

P. O. Box 1382, Lobatse

Tel: +267 7162 4001

Email: *tesbnm@gmail.com*

DEDICATION

To all torch bearers around the globe who devotes their moment in life to serve and heal the world.

FOREWORD

When it comes to matters of your life, and whether or not you will be able to influence what transpires in your daily life, you must always remember that all things begin with a thought. It is thoughts in your mind that grows into ideas about what is or what is not, and then generates a sense of feeling (good or bad) inside of you, which in turn determines your action, in response. If you want to influence good feelings, and ultimately positive action on your part, you must begin by opening-up to positive words of wisdom and interact with positively-inclined people whose thoughts are enriched with life-enhancing ideas. The simplest way is to invest in books on personal development and growth, so you can give yourself an opportunity to learn from a wide range of lessons, and ultimately edit your own thoughts and develop new ideas.

Some two decades ago I read for the first time Susan Jeffer's book *Feel The Fear and Do It Anyway*, and got introduced to the aspect of a *Higher Self* that exists within every individual, and how this part of the human being is a source for positive thoughts and energy. I also learnt about the *Chatterbox*, representing the *Ego Self*, which only serves to distract one from what is real in terms of how to effectively advance their life. The main lesson I learnt is that in order to manifest your desires, you must connect with your *Higher Self*, through your subconscious mind, and present your thoughts about what you really want, as in making a wish, and then you will be presented with some opportunities to manifest that which you desire. While still pondering over the meaning of all these concepts i.e. higher self, subconscious mind etc., I stumbled into a book (so I thought then, but now I believe it was the universe responding) called *The Power Of The Subconscious Mind* by Dr.

Joseph Murphy, wherein I learnt about a powerful tool to cause for change through thoughts, termed *"scientific praying"*. The latter is a deliberate act to prefer and hold, for a prolonged period, the good thoughts and ideas about what you desire and intend to manifest in your life. In other words, instead of chit-chatting in your chatterbox and sending your mind on a wild-goose chase about what could be or what is not etc., you set your mind (with conviction or faith) on exactly that you desire or wish to manifest. This act then triggers a process in your subconscious mind to bring to your attention opportunities through-which you can find ways to manifest your desires.

Although I did not deliberately try-out the idea on *"scientific praying"*, after reading Dr. Murphy's book, I however became aware of certain experiences that affected me, and can easily be explained through the same idea.

While undertaking my doctorate study on Palynostratigraphy (Geology) in France, between 2001 and 2007, I often got stuck as I was doing a completely new subject that I had no prior experience on. Amazingly, I always seemed to find solutions whenever I put my mind to it. Whenever faced with a challenge, like how to present some of my data and results, I would begin to think a lot on possibilities, and then consult books as well as google, and ultimately after a day or so an idea just presents itself. This did not happen once or twice, but it happened several times until I completed my research. I however did not at the time think in terms of *"scientific praying"*, but it was only after some period that I began to make a link. I have no doubt today that the events as they unfolded during my study i.e. my organised and focused thoughts to seek for solutions, were a reflection of the idea explained in Dr. Murphy's book as *"scientific praying"*.

I now believe that the idea of one being able to influence what they desire through thoughts is something that is real not only for a few enlightened individuals but for everyone. The only difference is that those who are enlightened have become aware and are able to notice what they are presented with and how it links with their thought patterns. Since the days of my research I have had several experiences with this concept, during my daily life, in terms of finding things or help etc., including finding a parking space at a busy shopping complex. I have since read several books centred on the idea that it is indeed your thoughts that eventually influence what transpires in your life, and a few of some of the greatest authors on this subject whose books I have read, include James Allen, Louise Hay, Dr. Wayne Dyer, Robert Holden etc. I put together this little book, therefore, with the intention to present you with several possibilities to influence your thought patterns, so you can begin to create new ideas and eventually transform your life. I hope you find this a worthy course.

Kind regards,

Dr. Benson N. Modie

CONSIDER FIRST WHAT YOU CAN DO FOR YOURSELF

Instead of wallowing in thoughts about what is bad that others have done or not done in your life, you can change your thoughts and begin to think about what matters most to you......and then consider the little things you can do for yourself now. This way you give your life momentum and a sense of new beginning, as you get back on track along your preferred direction of the journey of your life. The little steps you can take by yourself may include simply going out to seek for help and learn from the experiences of others, as well as reading books to augment your level of understanding......and making sure that you act on advice obtained.

These may initially seem just little and ineffective steps but in the longer term you will realise much improvement in your handling and management of the journey of your life.   Most importantly, you will develop the habit of positive self-talk, which will work to boost your confidence in self-belief, as well as raise your level of self-esteem.   Be aware that wherever you are now is not the end of the journey of your life…..you can still go the extra mile and experience greater fulfilment. But first you must train your mind to think only positive thoughts.

SORT-OUT YOUR MENTAL CLUTTER

Learn to sort-out your mental clutter and get rid of the "trivial many" thoughts you host in your mind. According to the Pareto Principle or the 20/80 Rule only 20% of the thoughts you host in your mind will yield 80% of the results you desire in your life. This 20% of productive thoughts are referred to as the "vital few", while the 80% of wasteful thoughts are called the "trivial many".

Many of us consider the thoughts we have as being outside of our control, as they may seem overwhelming most of the time. However, each of us has the power to choose what to think and what not to think…..and all you need to do is to begin to tame your self-talk…..and let your mind know who is in charge. Become aware of your negative thoughts and self-talk, and make a conscious decision to disallow them a free-role in your mind.....as they are just a source of anarchy and disorder in your life.

You need to take full control of your mind.....it is the only way to influence the conditions of peace, love, joy and happiness, along your journey of life. Remember that you are a natural living being.....you are not artificial......and you have access to the same power that created all that is nature. Think positive and trust in your natural ability to manage well any life situation that comes before you.

SEEK TO MAKE CONSCIOUS CONTACT WITH YOUR DIVINE-SELF

Allow yourself to think and imagine the early days when you were conceived. Would you say the natural process (or divine intelligence) that put together all the pieces to create a living being out of you was a struggle? It is the same process that drove and secured your growth throughout early childhood…..and the same process is still operational inside of you the same way as before…..to sustain your growth and continued existence in life.

What seems to have now changed is that your human life practices, largely dominated by artificial life styles, have succeeded to distract and detach you from your natural source of being. Now you see yourself as a separate and independent being that must work hard and struggle, in order to make it in life…..despite the fact that you have this endless power within you, which you have totally forgotten about (or you are just ignorant about it). This way of life (i.e. hard work and struggle) unfortunately has never been effective anywhere, as it has not managed to yield any long term results, with regard to the human life desires of peace, love, joy and happiness. The struggle way of living is the way of the ego-self, which essentially is a complete opposite of your natural or true-self (i.e. divine-self) way that does not limit nor control your advancement and growth in life.

To get back on track then think of the early days when you were created....and believe that the same process that made and nurtured you from early childhood remains readily available throughout your entire life. Refrain from a life of struggles and worries....and just be in-sync with the divine intelligence that got you here. It is the same intelligence that brings out joyous art, music, talent, creativity etc., through many people of the world.....and many more human life co-creations.

EMBRACE THE DIVERSITY IN HUMAN LIFE PRACTICES AND PREFERENCES

Promote in your mind thought patterns that embraces the diversity in human life practices and preferences. Get your mind to appreciate the differences in the levels of understanding between people…..and that such differences is often the cause of our (i.e. us people) inability to relate well with others. Think less of the differences between you and others but more of the areas of common interest. In the event you sense a difference in thought patterns between you and others, just acknowledge the difference, and make a pronouncement to the effect you respect the views of others, and that however, you see things differently.

BECOME AWARE THAT GOD HAS NO FAVOURITES BUT THAT ONLY YOUR WORTH COUNTS

Get it into your mind that God has no favourites….and that you too are just as important as anyone else or any other natural creation you can think of. What may set you apart from others is your value to life or how much worthy you have made yourself to be to life. Think of yourself as having been created to serve certain roles during your moment of existence….with the aim to add value to life.

Allow your mind to be dominated by thoughts that only urges you to contribute something for the good of humanity, as in there lies your chance to ignite the conditions of peace, love, joy and happiness…..for you and for all of humanity. This is what we ought to be doing to improve our human relations, and create an opportunity to ultimately heal the world.

WORK YOUR WAY OUT OF THE TENDENCY TO BLAME AND COMPLAIN ENDLESSLY

Begin to slowly work your thought patterns away from the non-productive tendency to blame and complain endlessly. Instead, think of all people as opportunities....in a positive way...as in the saying "no man is an island". Have a mind-set that views all partnerships between people as a form of synergy.....with the aim to give each other momentum, or a little push, along the journey of life so that we can each reach our visions. Instead of just complaining and blaming......and running the risk of turning everyone against you.....think of how you can ask for help, and even learn, from others. Remember that it is your journey of life and you must travel it, while others can only assist where you ask not when you complain and blame.

CULTIVATE THOUGHTS THAT ARE GENTLE AND FLEXIBLE BUT POWERFUL LIKE WATER

Cultivate in your mind thoughts that are gentle and flexible like water....and yet so powerful and strong like when water turns a whole mountain into sand in a river bed. Gentle thoughts in your mind carry the power to build and construct while the hard and tough-guy thoughts tend to be destructive and devoid of love. Only a gentle mind is capable of thinking peace, love, joy and happiness, and knows what it means to respect the being in others. A gentle and calm mind is a conduit for strong and flexible diplomatic ties between opposing factions of human life support sectors, and hence a great opportunity to setting the foundation to improving human relations and overall world peace.

RECOGNISE AND REWARD ALL YOUR ACHIEVEMENTS NO MATTER HOW LITTLE THEY ARE

Instead of overwhelming your mind with thoughts of being not successful in life, begin to identify specific moments where you did well in the past, no matter how little you achieved......and no matter how fewer people or no one at all acknowledges such. Think of these little moments of achievement as indicators to the potential you have to go the extra mile and achieve much more than you can imagine.

Respond to these indicators by raising your awareness level and the ability to recognise any future accomplishments in your life. Then learn to give yourself a little reward....even if it is just a pat on the back....each time you recognise a sign of achievement by yourself. From now onwards disable the thought process that always seeks to compare you with those deemed to be more successful than you. Instead enable the thinking that those who are where they are, in success, also started somewhere.....and that you too will get over there sometime, if you put your mind to it.

REMAIN MINDFUL AND RESPECTFUL OF INTER-PERSONAL DIFFERENCES BETWEEN PEOPLE

When interacting with others, on your daily life engagements, always remain mindful of the fact that people are at different levels of awareness, understanding, experience, interests, desires etc. Such is what will determine the extent and quality of your human relations…..and whether or not the partnerships you engage-in are fruitful. The bottom-line though is to acknowledge and respect the being in others, and lead yourself in the direction of your preference.

You however need not despair as there will always be a small percentage of those heading in the same direction as you are…..and this is where you are likely to get the most support in productive human interactions.

CULTIVATE THE HABIT OF READING SELF-HELP LITERATURE TO WEED-OFF UNPRODUCTIVE THOUGHTS

If you find that your mind is often cluttered with unproductive thoughts......and most of the time you feel overwhelmed and unable to make progress doing what you really want.....your best way out of this predicament is to cultivate a habit of reading. The best reads would be books from the self-help categories of body-mind-spirit, motivation and inspiration, and personal development and life planning etc. Reading this type of literature will help you dwarf any negative unproductive thoughts that may have been renting your mental space, as you begin to fill that space with new and exciting thoughts.

You will begin to notice and appreciate many different ways that you could adopt to give momentum to your journey of life. You will no longer feel that you are stuck doing the same things and getting the same results, but instead you will begin to see opportunities where you didn't see any before. The reason being that you now think differently......a change of thoughts.......and most importantly, you now feel powerful, than powerless, to be able to manage any life challenges that comes before you. Isn't that quality growth?

TO HAVE A GREATER IMPACT IN LIFE YOU MUST FINE-TUNE YOURSELF TO CONNECT WITH THE DIVINE FREQUENCY

Think of a radio appliance that brings you news and music from anywhere around the globe where there is some radio signals. What you need for your radio to function effectively.....and bring you closer to the world through your favourite radio presenters.....is to connect it to a power supply. Now it is up to you to tune into whatever signal or frequency you desire, so you can listen to your favourite radio station. If you are not able to fine-tune your radio then you are not going to have a good reception.....and your radio will not be clear for you to enjoy the programme on air. Sometimes you might have to move a distance from where you are to get a better signal so you can get a clear reception on your radio. Depending on how well your radio can pick-up the broadcast frequency from your favourite radio, you may find that signals from other radio stations interferes with yours, creating some noise and making it difficult to follow what your radio station is broadcasting.

Much like the radio metaphor above, human beings must also be fine-tuned, in order to pick-up the divine signal that will allow for their completeness and effectiveness in life. First, the human body, like the radio appliance, must be supplied with energy through food and oxygen. This will give the body physical ability and mental capacity to search for and connect with the divine intelligence (i.e. frequency) that exists everywhere in the universe. Once the individual is linked-up or tuned to the divine frequency then you have a true human being, with access to an endless supply of divine power. This is when you are anchored on that gentle little person or inner-child that exist inside of you…..and always assuring, forgiving and positive.

Now, the moment you interact with worldly external factors, including other humans tuned to different frequencies, you begin to experience a great deal of noise and interference…….and that is when you stumble out of your divine frequency range. At this point you have lost your divine signal and you are anchored on your ego-self, where you begin to engage in endless contests and conflicts with others. In other words everyone around you (cf. radio stations) tries to broadcast their thoughts and ideas through you…..and you feel the need to defend your position. You can always get yourself out of this situation by fine-tuning yourself to find the divine frequency i.e. the voice of your inner-child, which will reconnect you with your divine source. To stay connected, you must make sure to believe and obey this little voice of your inner-child, then no other outside frequencies will encroach into your zone. Know that all humans have this weakness to lose their divine signal along the journey of life, but equally, all humans have the ability to fine-tune and find their divine frequency.

BOOST YOUR HUMAN LIFE EXPERIENCE BY DEVELOPING A HOLISTIC WELLNESSS MAINTENANCE PLAN

If you really love to experience human life in the best form possible you must begin by learning how to grow whole. The latter entails learning to understand the basic components of a human being i.e. the body, the mind, and the spirit, and how these must synergize to give you the highest level of effectiveness in your human form. Keep it in mind at all times that although your "spirit" is your divine-self, or your link to God, and is forever eternal.......as well as being ageless, formless, and timeless......your "body" however is the determinant factor of your human form. In other words, whether or not you will exist in the form of a human being that is able to relate with others through the five senses of sight, hearing, touch, smell, and taste, it is your body that can make that possible. Your body is the vehicle, the shelter, the tool etc., through which your spirit can fulfil your worth in human life. In addition, your body also provides a secure locality to house your mind, and hence your intelligence and intellect......which allows you to manage yourself well in human life. Let it sync with your human mind that once your body becomes dysfunctional, by whatever causes, then your moment in human life is over.

So, if you really love human life now is the time to develop for yourself a growing-whole wellness maintenance plan. The latter will ensure that you develop and grow spiritually, so that you are able to utilise your divine energy to live your worth and add value to life. Your wellness maintenance plan must also cater for the nurturance and development of your mental growth, through acts that deliberately fosters the habit of continuous and life-long learning. This way you will have a strong, well-informed and determined mind that knows how to make choices and decisions that can advance your course in life, and ultimately make it possible for you to create the future you desire, despite all other circumstances of life.

Lastly, and most importantly, your wellness maintenance plan must be deliberately designed to ensure daily practices (i.e. healthy habits) that cater for the upkeep of your body for longevity. Yes, if you can learn how to grow whole......and act it.......you will have the best moment of your human life, and ultimately you can go back as a fulfilled and delighted spiritual being.

BE CONTENT WITH WHO YOU ARE AS THAT FORMS AN EXTENSION OF GOD'S OWN PERFECT CREATION

Cleanse your mind of any thoughts that considers you as being imperfect simply because of some perceived failure, weaknesses or poor judgements on your part by others. Begin now to learn and appreciate that all of nature, inclusive of you, represents God's own perfect creation. Develop a habit to pay attention to all forms of nature around you e.g. plants, animals, landforms, cosmic bodies etc., and recognize that all exhibits a wide range of diversity in form within their group. Hence, the fact that you may look different, think otherwise, prefer and choose differently, try several times before you can succeed etc., is just naturally perfect and should not make you think like you are "the odd one out".

Your weaknesses, mistakes, poor judgments etc., are all part of a naturally perfect and evolving being. The only thing you must concern yourself with.....as opposed to worrying about the expectations and judgments of others......is whether or not you are learning from your experiences and growing from it, so as to improve your effectiveness in taking part in life i.e. living.   Keep the following words ingrained in your mind; you were never meant to be how others would like you to be, instead you were meant to be how you desire to be.

ASSUME THE LEAD ROLE OF THE JOURNEY OF YOUR LIFE

Populate your mind with thoughts that encourages you to be proactive and at-cause, so you can always be in the lead role of the journey of your life. This way you get to ensure that you maintain the bearing to your vision.......as well as making sure that you act to get your journey in motion. You do not have to wait for something or someone to get you where you want to be, instead you must get yourself there while you still have plenty of time (i.e. to falter, to fall etc., and get up and go....!), and others will come to your assist along the way as you maintain focus on what matters most to you about your life.

Do not get discouraged at the early stages when things do not seem to take-off as well as you would like......and avoid to indulge in disappointment when others do not live up to your expectations. Just simply feel the disappointment and learn from the experience, but develop a strong resolve to get you there. The more you learn the more knowledge you accumulate in your mind.....and the wiser you become, and hence you can transform your thoughts and believe systems.....and ultimately all acts become less and less difficult to undertake. This is when you become crystal clear about what you want and how you are going to make it happen.....and you know that come-what-may, you are getting yourself there.

BECOME AWARE THAT YOU ONLY HAVE A FIXED AMOUNT OF TIME TO UTILIZE IN YOUR HUMAN FORM

Cultivate in your mind the thinking that it is time rather than money that is critical to your existence in life. Learn to appreciate the fact that while money can be made any time and any day, time available can only be used once but never made again. If you lose money today you can always make plans to make some tomorrow. But if you lose the time provided today you are never getting it back tomorrow......and you cannot make any........instead you have to use tomorrow's time for today's blunders. That essentially means that your moment to live for today has been wasted and you remain with fewer days to live. You only have a fixed amount of time available to utilize over your life span.

If you continue to be inefficient with time provided, you may end-up having to leave without having lived or being purposeful in life, as your time comes to an end. The money race never ends and it can steal your entire moment to live.....but you have to be smart and make plans to remain purposeful in your daily life engagements.

TAKE CHARGE OF YOUR MIND TO STREAMLINE AND ORGANISE YOUR SELF-TALK

You must take charge of your mind so that you manage your self-talk. If you allow your mind to go blah blah blah all day and all night long about what others are saying or not saying about you….doing or not doing for you….or even what you are doing or not doing, you will lose out on your time to do what matters most to life. You will certainly spend sleepless nights and not get as much rest as you need to prepare for the next day, and you will surely drop down on your productivity level at the workplace. Worse still, chances are you will lose focus and grip on life and never get fulfilled in your human life experience.

But you can change all that if you like, by first introducing new and positive thoughts and ideas into your mind…..and making sure that your mind is under your control and does not just engage in any and every thoughts that do not advance your course in life.

ALWAYS SEE YOURSELF AS A VALUABLE AND INDISPENSABLE PART OF HUMAN LIFE

Always maintain a positive mind about your being and your worth in life......and see yourself all the time as a valuable and indispensable part of human life. Think of your purpose in life and how you could make every moment count by engaging in acts that add value to life in general. Remain mindful of the fact that your days in this human form are numbered, and hence you cannot afford to waste a moment on what matters not or simply just stuck in endless procrastination escapades.

Ask yourself, how could I be relevant to life......everyday.....every moment? What is my worth to life? What little things can I do that can help.....at home.....at the workplace.....the community......or the world? Know that you are a pulse of unlimited renewable energy, and if you cannot engage in something worthy to life then all that energy goes to waste without any trace.........and your existence in life remains a love gift in vain.

TO BE SUCCESSFUL YOU MUST BE PATIENT AND PAY ATTENTION TO DETAILS ABOUT EDUCATION

If you learn to be patient and pay attention to details about education........and its profound effect in shaping the quality of life for any individual......you will begin to appreciate that the time to live is after-all long enough for you to manifest your desires. The earlier you embrace learning the better, as you will develop a better understanding of the need to put order and organisation in your life, if you are to create that sense of a memorable life experience for yourself.

Paying attention to education will help you gain insight on the need to deliberately learn to upgrade your mental system, so that you know better how to make effective decisions......as well as making the right choices in life. By adopting a habit of continuous and life-long learning, you will develop to appreciate the meaning of purposeful living....and the need to undertake the process of envisioning, in order to put form to the future you desire. Thereafter, all acts of your learning will be streamlined toward fulfilling your purpose, and making your vision a reality.

All this will take a life-time, but will be characterised by a life of meaning and worth, and hence will allow you to create the conditions of peace, love, joy and happiness, along the journey of your life. Ultimately, you will be totally spent.....as you would have exhausted all your abilities and worth to add value to life…..and it will be time to get back home.

YOU ARE NATURAL AND POWERFUL, AND YOU WERE NEVER MEANT TO STRUGGLE IN LIFE

One thing you must become aware of, and always remember no matter what difficulties you may go through, is that you are natural rather than artificial, and that nature never struggles. When you were introduced into life on earth, the expectation was that you would learn and know how to use your natural power to manifest your desires, instead of just choosing to struggle......and hoping that things will get better some-day, somehow. The Sun does not struggle to rise and illuminate the entire Earth even when the Moon distract by coming in-between to cause an eclipse......instead the Sun continues to use its natural power to rise and by-pass the Moon, to be in a better position to continue to give more light to Planet Earth and its inhabitants. Planet Earth on the other hand has been hugely scarred by anthropogenic processes (i.e. man-caused artificial processes) but still continues to function naturally to re-modify its landscapes.

Learn and understand that the same natural force that operates within the Sun, the Moon, and the Planet Earth, is the same natural life-force that exists inside of you.......and that force does not die, nor end, nor become exhausted.......but is always available to you to modify your life in a way you desire. Things only begin to really go wrong in your life, as a natural being, when you give-up on learning, and you deny yourself the opportunity to understand and know-how, but instead choose to just expect from other natural beings like you. If you want a better life experience you must get back to your natural-self...........like when you were still a kid, full of enthusiasm and with endless ideas of creativity.......and you made use of your natural power to create your own toys and games. You have the natural power to create valuable and worthy landmarks out of your desires, and become purposely fulfilled in life.

TO FEEL GOOD, LEARN, ENVISION AND ACT TO MANIFEST THE FUTURE YOU DESIRE

Train your mind to think, imagine and envision..........and see yourself living the kind of life you desire to experience. Get it stuck in your mind that the only thing that matters most during your life-time is whether or not you are feeling good in life..........and hence succeeding in living a memorable life experience. Learn to appreciate the basic fact that life is as is, and it is the same for everyone, and that for you to feel good you must act to cause the results you desire in your life. If you are not feeling good in your life, it is because you have not made much effort to learn and understand yourself......and then learn about life......and ultimately act on what you know to influence the outcome of your experience of life.

Learn to understand that there certainly are many ways to different forms of success, but there is only one way to real success, which is purposeful living, and that way is through the path of education and personal development. If you do not understand yourself you will never know what is good for you, and hence you will never feel any good for any length of period. If you do not learn to upgrade your level of understanding in life then you will never know how much ability you have to create the future you desire, and hence you will never be fulfilled in life. If you still have hope to feel good in life, now is the time to get back to learning ways and make a turn toward the future you desire.

Remember, there is absolutely nothing you can do better or good outside of understanding and knowing, or simply by the way of short-cuts and trial-and-error. Get real, learn first, and act on knowledge acquired, then the future is all yours to manifest.

TO ADVANCE YOUR LIFE YOU NEED TO LOOK WITHIN TO RECLAIM YOUR POWER FOR BEING

If you desire stability and advancement in your own life, you need not look any further than within to find solutions to your situations in life. To overly rely on others, with the expectation that they will somehow create favourable situations for you, is simply giving away your power to determine and manifest the future you desire. The solution to any situation that may come your way must come from within you, firstly because it is your situation that needs to be solved, and in a way that addresses needs as defined by you, and secondly because it is your life desire, rather than those others you may expect from, and most importantly you are host to unlimited eternal power, readily available for utilisation any moment you choose so.

Others can only assist, advise, coach, teach or give a little helping hand etc., but you must take complete charge and leadership of the journey of your life. Remember, you have the key to turn-on that magnificent power inside of you to create the momentum that will drive you and your life in the direction of your preference. No one else has access to that key but you.....and it is so for everyone else. Hence, to overly rely on others and expect them to shape your life for you (i.e. essentially live your life on your behalf).........and even complain about it when they don't.........is like turning your back on your creator, and refusing to utilise that unlimited and free-for-all power within, to engage in meaningful and purposeful activities that serve life. So, what are you here for then?

EPILOGUE

Human life is currently wobbling more than ever before and I bet it is nothing closer to anything you ever imagined during your toddler days. All we get to see and hear nowadays is bad news after bad news of all sorts all the time.....and it seems endlessly relentless. What are we not doing right? This certainly is not the best way to express our gratitude for the gift of life. I know that much of the world population, like myself, is not at all amused by the current trends in human relations, and would prefer to see a more organised, united, focused, effective and advancing human species. Disappointing as things may seem I however believe that humanity has all the power to cause for change in the desired way, and it is something that we can all influence beginning at our individual levels. If you and I, as individuals, resolve to commit in a positive way, to our daily engagements in life, no doubt we can cause a change and bring stability to the turmoil that is becoming modern day human life.

Don't say "well, it's not my fault", or "but the government must do something", or "it's up to the world leaders to figure out something" etc. You too have a role to play, and that is part of the reason "why you are here".......and you of course have to start by learning how to engage in life through purposeful and meaningful ways. I believe that if we can all decide to do something positive every day which adds value to life then we can influence those around us to shift their focus from negative acts that only serve to destroy human life, and instead begin to appreciate a way of life that draws from ones worth and purposeful engagements. To reach this level of thinking, in an already toxic human life system, requires a great deal of motivation and inspiration to re-take that earlier first step of the journey of education and human development. It is only through the acquisition of new knowledge into our mind system that we can begin to think different and better thoughts, as well as create wonderful life-nurturing ideas about the future of human life.

Please join me, through this book, and billions of other peace-loving and peace-seeking individuals around the globe in sharing our knowledge, experience, stories etc., with the aim to bring stability to human life. Make it a habit to visit a learning forum, book store etc., near where you are, to allow yourself an opportunity to learn something new so that you can improve your contributions to life in general. I have no doubt in my mind that you too would love to see a better world for all of humanity than the world we live in today. Always remember that despite our differences in thoughts, views, opinions, preferences, interests etc., our common vision as humanity is a world engulfed in peace, love, joy and happiness.......and it can only happen if we all learn and act right.

For more on motivation and personal development go to:

www.worldsmostexoticblog.blogspot.com

www.facebook.com/cfkbw

Made in the USA
Columbia, SC
13 June 2024

35936921R00039